KATE RIGGS

grow with me

BEE

CREATIVE EDUCATION

Published by Creative Education
P.O. Box 227, Mankato, Minnesota 56002
Creative Education is an imprint of
The Creative Company
www.thecreativecompany.us

Design and production by Ellen Huber
Art direction by Rita Marshall
Printed in the United States of America

Photographs by Alamy (Scott Camazine, Corbis Cusp,
FLPA, Papilio, WILDLIFE GmbH, David Wootton),
Bigstock (mbagdon, photoprof), Dreamstime (Andrey
Davidenko, Dave Massey), Getty Images (Ingo Arndt,
Stephen Dalton, Steve Hopkin, Heidi & Hans-Juergen
Koch, Thomas Lottermoser, Pete Oxford, Visuals
Unlimited, Inc./Eric Tourneret, John Woodcock,
Konrad Wothe), iStockphoto (malerapaso), Shutterstock
(Subbotina Anna, jocic, kesipun, D. Kucharski &
K. Kucharska, Peter Waters), SuperStock (Minden
Pictures), Wikipedia (Waugsberg)

Library of Congress Cataloging-in-Publication Data
Riggs, Kate.
Bee / Kate Riggs.
p. cm. — (Grow with me)
Includes bibliographical references and index.
Summary: An exploration of the life cycle and life
span of bees, using up-close photographs and step-
by-step text to follow a honeybee's growth process
from egg to larva to pupa to mature insect.

ISBN 978-1-60818-214-5
1. Honeybee—Life cycles—Juvenile literature. I. Title.
QL568.A6R543 2012
595.799—dc23   2011040495

CPSIA: 021413 PO1656
9 8 7 6 5 4 3 2

TABLE OF CONTENTS

Honeybees are insects. Insects have six legs and one or two pairs of wings. Bees have just one pair of wings. Their wings and legs are connected to the part of their body called the **thorax**.

head

thorax

abdomen

4

Bees live together in large groups called colonies. There can be as many as 50,000 bees in a colony! Each colony lives in a **hive**, or nest. In the wild, bees usually make their nests in hollow trees. Sometimes they nest in caves or between rocks, too.

This bee colony built a hive in a gap in a rotted tree.

5

Drones mate with the queen bee so that she can make eggs. Then the drones die.

6

queen bee   *drone*   *worker bee*

There is one **queen bee** in every colony. All the other female bees are called **worker bees**. All the male bees are called **drones**. There are many more worker bees than drones.

Worker bees eat a lot of **honey** to make **beeswax**. The wax comes from four **glands** under each bee's **abdomen**. The workers use the wax to make **honeycombs**.

7

A worker bee has a sharp, pointed body part called a stinger. It can hurt people or other animals.

8 Honeycombs are where the queen bee lays her eggs. The queen is the only bee that can lay eggs. She can lay up to 2,000 eggs in a day!

The worker bees group together to warm up the hive while the queen lays her eggs. Beehives need to be about 93 °F (34 °C) at all times. Bees are cold-blooded. This means they cannot keep their bodies warm if the temperature around them is not also warm.

Young worker bees are sometimes called "house bees" because they stay in the hive.

9

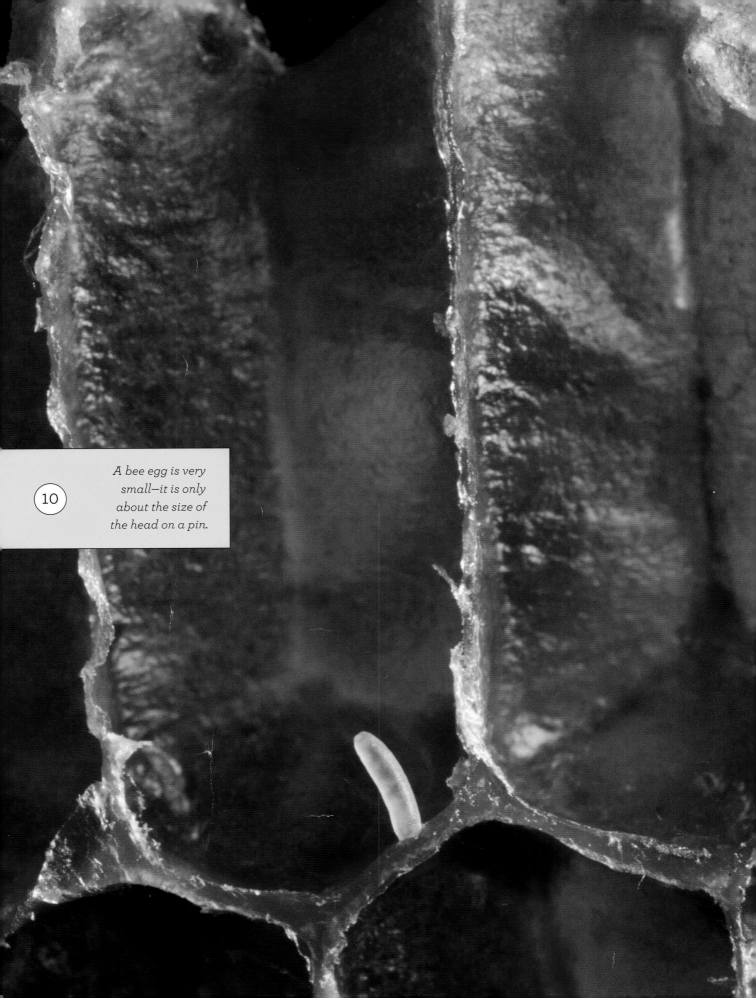

A bee egg is very small—it is only about the size of the head on a pin.

Each tiny bee egg attaches to the bottom of a honeycomb **cell**. As soon as it is laid, the egg starts to change. Inside, a bee **larva** is growing.

The egg hatches after three days, and the bee larva crawls out. The larva is white in color and about as long as a grain of rice. It has no wings, legs, or eyes. It has only a mouth.

11

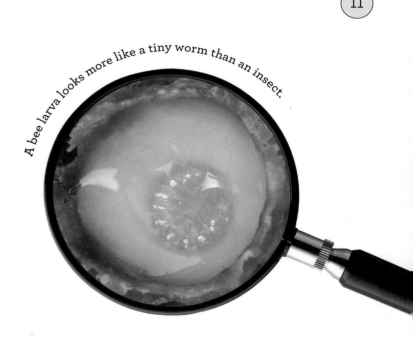

A bee larva looks more like a tiny worm than an insect.

The small larva floats on a pool of **royal jelly** in the cell. Worker bees feed royal jelly to the larva.

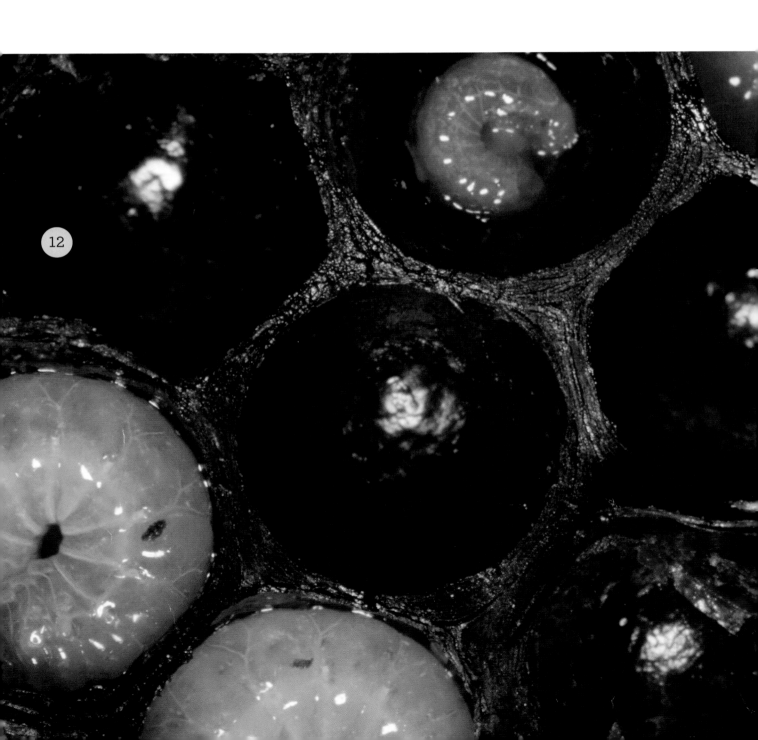

12

A large beehive can have as many as 10,000 larvae growing in it. Most of the larvae will become worker bees. A hive needs many worker bees.

Worker bee larvae eat up the royal jelly quickly. They do not float in it for long.

13

A bee uses a part of its back legs called the pollen basket to collect pollen.

(14) The worker bees feed royal jelly to the larva for about three days. Then they start giving the larva honey and **pollen** from flowers instead.

The workers feed the larva more than 1,000 times a day for the next 5 or 6 days. The larva grows bigger and bigger. It sheds its skin five times as its body gets bigger.

Sometimes people grow bee larvae in a lab to study them.

15

The larva is fully grown eight days after it hatches. It is so big that it fills the cell. Its mouth faces the cell entrance. But the larva does not need any more food.

16

The workers close the cell with a cap of wax. The cap lets some air through. This helps the larva breathe.

Some of the cells in this hive have a white, waxy cap on them.

17

When the cell is sealed, the larva starts to change into a **pupa**. In three days, the larva sheds its skin again. This will be the last time.

A full-grown larva

18

Underneath the old skin is a pupa inside a pupal case. At first, the pupa looks like a soft bee without wings. Most of the hive's pupae grow into worker bees in the next 10 days. Drones take a few days longer.

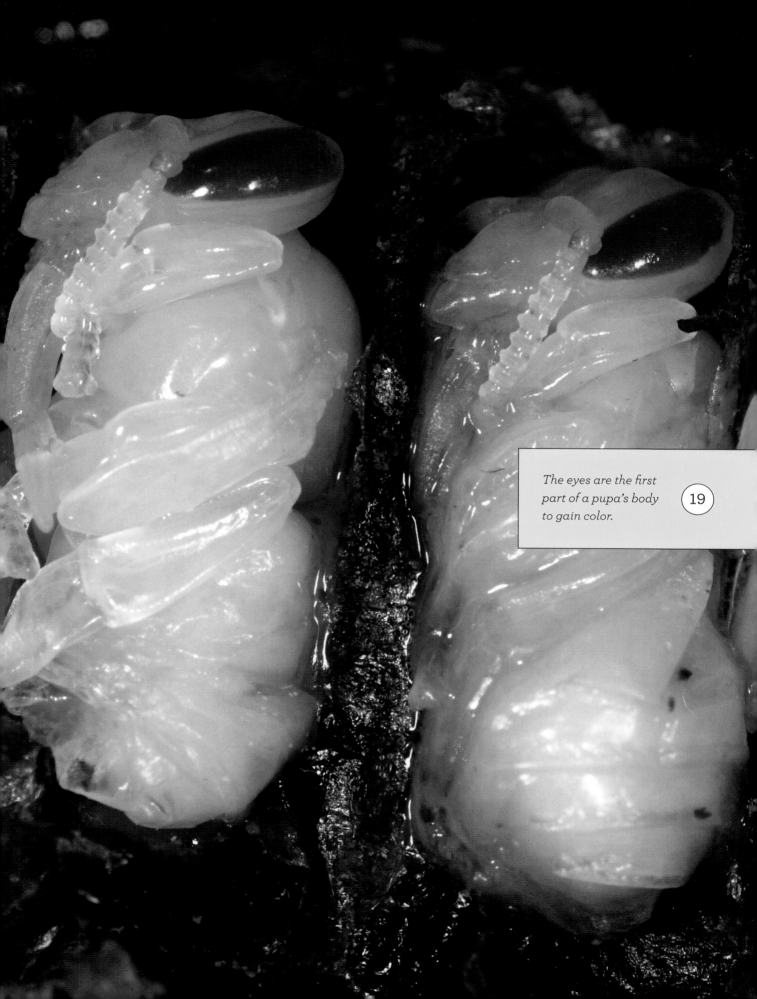

The eyes are the first part of a pupa's body to gain color.

19

Two antennae stick out of a bee's head. They help the bee touch, taste, and smell.

20

By day 10, the pupa changes color. Its eyes are dark, and it has wings now. The pupa chews its way through the cap and out of the cell. It leaves the pupal case behind.

The new worker bee's body is still soft, and its wings are squashed. After a day, its body hardens, and its wings straighten out. Now it can fly.

After bee wings harden,
they can beat 400 to
450 times per minute.

21

Bees can live for only one summer. So if a worker bee is born in the summer, it lives only about six weeks. For the first two to three weeks, the young worker will stay in the hive. It helps keep the honeycomb cells clean. It also helps feed the queen, the larvae, and the drones.

(22) *A bee gathers pollen from the part of a flower called the stamen.*

Worker bees start leaving the hive when they are three to four weeks old. They eat a lot of honey before they leave. This gives them energy to fly around looking for pollen and **nectar** in flowers.

The bee shown in the middle uses the waggle dance to talk to other workers.

24

Other worker bees tell the young bee where to find food. They dance in front of the bee. The movements in the dance tell the bee where it needs to go! Bees fly to many different flowers on warm, sunny days.

The worker bee collects pollen on its back legs to take back to the hive. It also carries pollen to one flower from another. When the bee lands on a flower, it **pollinates** the flower. Now the flower can form seeds.

25

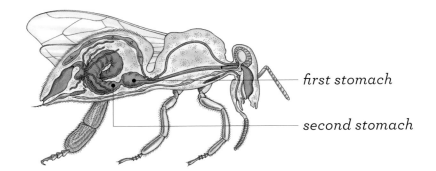

first stomach

second stomach

Bees have two stomachs. One is just for collecting nectar. A bee gets nectar from 100 to 1,500 flowers to fill up its "honey stomach." Then it goes back to the hive.

Some people keep bees in beehives so that they can collect the honey.

A bee uses a long mouthpart called a proboscis (pro-BAH-sis) to suck up nectar.

Other worker bees take the nectar and chew it for about 30 minutes. Then they store it in empty honeycomb cells. The nectar dries into a thick syrup. It becomes honey! When a cell is full, worker bees seal it with wax.

A queen bee grows in a cell that hangs from the honeycomb and is called a queen cup.

28 The workers feed the queen bee all the time so she can keep laying eggs. She lays fewer eggs as she gets older. A queen lives only about two years. When she is ready to die, she lays an egg in a larger cell. The workers feed only royal jelly to the larva in that cell. This larva will become the hive's next queen.

A sealed queen cup can be large. It gives the bigger queen room to gro[w]

29

The queen bee lays her eggs  in the honeycomb cells.

A larva begins growing in the egg.

The larva hatches from the egg in 3 days.

The larva sheds its skin 5 times.

30

At 8 days old, the larva is  fully grown.

 The larva changes into a pupa at about 11 days old.

A pupa grows for 10 days to become a worker bee.

The worker bee leaves the hive when it is 3 weeks old.

After about 3 weeks, the worker bee dies.

abdomen: *the third and last part of an insect's body, behind the head and thorax*

beeswax: *the wax that is made by bees' bodies and used to build honeycombs*

cell: *the part of the honeycomb where the queen bee lays an egg*

drones: *male bees; their job is to mate with the queen*

glands: *parts of animals' bodies that produce something, like wax*

hive: *the home or nest of bees*

honey: *a sweet, sticky food made by bees from the nectar of flowers*

honeycombs: *collections of wax cells formed by bees in a hive*

larva: *the form a bee takes after it hatches but before it has skin and wings; "larvae" is the word for more than one larva*

nectar: *a sweet, sugary liquid that flowers make*

pollen: *a yellow powder made by flowers that is used to fertilize other flowers*

pollinates: *takes pollen from one flower to another to fertilize the plant, causing seeds to grow*

pupa: *the form a bee takes as it changes from larva to adult; "pupae" is the word for more than one pupa*

queen bee: *the only female bee in the hive that lays eggs*

royal jelly: *a liquid produced by worker bees and fed to larvae*

thorax: *the middle part of an insect's body, between the head and the abdomen*

worker bees: *bees that make wax, care for the hive, feed the larvae and other bees, and collect pollen and nectar*

31

WEB SITES

Bee-aMazed Children's Garden: Activities for Kids
http://www.longwoodgardens.org/BeeAmazed.html
Download bee-related information and activities.

Tales from the Hive: Dances with Bees
http://www.pbs.org/wgbh/nova/bees/danceslang.html
Learn about the dances bees do, and try being a bee!

READ MORE

Cole, Joanna. *The Magic School Bus: Inside a Beehive.*
New York: Scholastic, 1996.

Micucci, Charles. *The Life and Times of the Honeybee.*
New York: Houghton Mifflin, 1995.

INDEX